BABYLON

Santa The Hot Ice — Sassy Preacher Of A Sexy Gospel.

Ebarim Fortune Godsend.

Foreword.

This book reveals some practices in the church which have been made to be superior to the laws of the Lord himself. Some doctrinal differences that exist today are still amendable only if we're willing.

Babylon is Santa's Empire, and Santa is the king of Babylon. He thrives by his means, the most useful of which is deception.

Watch! That's all I can say.

"Habits, once formed, either become our "god", or our devils. You might say that demons are responsible for your ordeals in life, but, it is truer that they only took advantage of, and thrived on your habits"".

Customs are habits. God is in them when they're good, and Satan is also in them when they're evil.

Meditate on that.

Dedication.

This piece of a great work is dedicated to the Almighty God through the Lord Jesus Christ, and all who'll read, and buy for those who can't.

They're our HEROES.

Table Of Contents.

Chapter 1

Introduction.

Sometime ago, a fifty years old man got married for the first time to a thirty eight years old lady.

The man got married at that age because he wanted to amass great wealth before marrying, since that was the condition set forth by the woman he loved and desired so dearly.

After wedding, their marriage was blessed with seven female children within eight years, all being single births. Due to his wife's initial inability to give birth to a male child, the man also had two male children born to him from his concubines; for he thought that their ages weren't favorable to them should he keep hoping that his dear wife will still give birth to a male child. Another reason was that the man feared that his wife might be enjoying his wealth with another man soon after his demise like Abigail in the Bible, since he had no male heir to his estates.

The man was full of Bible head knowledge accumulated over time, though, without practice.

Finally, God proved His kindness to the woman during their tenth marriage anniversary, for she conceived and gave birth to a male child. The woman, determined to raise the only son to have unfair advantage over his half brothers, decided to place it on exclusive breastfeeding for two whole years, which was followed by inclusive breastfeeding for another two years — making a total of four years. So, the boy was breastfed for four years. Also, the woman fed the son through feeding bottles for another six years. The child became a professional sucker at this age.

The child was a well trained sucker, who will not depart from sucking his entire lifetime in fulfilment of the Scripture which says "train up a child in the way he should go: and when he is old, he will not depart from it". Proverbs 22:6.

The child's name was Solomon.

He resorted to feeding on his fingers since the mother would no longer breastfeed, nor "bottle-feed" him — he began to "finger feed" himself until he was twenty five years old, as nature aborts vacuum. Something else must be used instead!

Whenever he was jilted by his peers for sucking his left thumb, his response will always be that his dear mother raised him to be a sucker, and that he grew up sucking, and that he can't depart from it now that he's growing old because he loved God so much. He vowed to grow and live the way the mother trained him, so he won't incur God's wrath. He found solace in lollipops whenever he wasn't sucking his left thumb.

Solomon, being the Isaac of the house, as he was the only son of the married woman, other sons received the portion of Hagar, and Kethurah's sons. Genesis 25:5,6; was played out live by this wealthy family!

Solomon Is Married.

When Solomon was twenty five years old, his parents got him married to a very virtuous, beautiful, dutiful, intelligent, lovely, and god fearing lady.

Their marriage was so blessed that they had fifteen female children within sixteen years of marriage, all single births. Not even a set of twins.

That's record breaking. He doubled his parents' record.

Santa Is Born.

Mr. Solomon is our neighbor in the city, and we're close family friends. And I know that he's a very god fearing man, as much as the wife; and that they love each other so deeply that nothing will come in between them. Mr. Solomon, unlike his late father won't seek alternatives outside marriage.

However, we didn't know that his childhood training which became a habit composed a permanent prayer subject to his wife. Do you recall the habit, or you want to be reminded?

Mr. Solomon requested that I pray for the wife to conceive and give birth to a son since I was a dignified Prophet, which I did. And God was merciful by honoring my prayer for them that his wife conceived and gave birth to a son the following year. Their joy was ineffable as it knew no bounds. All in the neighborhood were summoned to join in their mirth.

The first son being the sixteenth son of the family was born in the seventeenth year of Mr. Solomon's marriage.

Mr. Solomon's wife name is Sister Mary.

The same day, Mr. Solomon requested that Sister Mary should give him assurance by vowing to bestow on their son twice as much care as he got from his mother when he was born! Sister Mary being so naïve consented to Mr. Solomon's demands, probably because she was excited, only to discover the details of Mr. Solomon's childhood later from her mother-in-law.

Amongst others, Sister Mary was informed that his dear husband was breastfed exclusively for two years, and inclusively for another two years, making up four years of breastfeeding. More so, she got to know that her lovely husband was bottle-fed for six years. He grew up sucking all his lifetime, including sucking his left thumb, and what follows soon.Mr. Solomon had been sucking unabashedly for twenty five years before getting married to Sister Mary.

So, Sister Mary having been made to know her husband's childhood training, turned to Mr. Solomon, in the presence of his mother and I ,said: "honey, that means I will stop breastfeeding you , since I have to breastfeed Santa (he was christened Santa since he was born on a Christmas day) for eight years. Four years exclusive breastfeeding and another four years of inclusive breastfeeding"; to double Mr. Solomon's record according to their earlier agreement. Mr. Solomon was to pay a price if the agreement will be valid and enforceable.

While I and Mr. Solomon's mother were working assiduously to recover from shock having heard that Mr. Solomon has been sucking until that moment, Sister Mary added, saying: "honey, I know that you'll understand! There's nothing to loose since Santa is your only son, and you really want him to get from me double of all that your mother ever gave to you — after all, I have committedly breastfed you everyday these past seventeen years"!

The foregoing led to Mr. Solomon's mother being comatose immediately, while I feigned not hearing what Sister Mary just said concerning her husband's lifelong habitual sucking.

The Power Of Early Child Training.

Mr. Solomon's response was that his habit was a direct effect of childhood training. That his dear mother raised him to be what he was at the time, and that she loved his mother so dearly for inculcating such values into his childhood training. Now, do you see why it's good to train a child in the way he should go?

Mr. Solomon's mother having been resuscitated from her coma, asked to know if Sister Mary's assertion were mere accusations or true, with regards to Mr. Solomon's daily breastfeeding program. Mr. Solomon responded by saying that that was the result of early child training, because the child will grow never departing from it, except such was a poor fool. He added that he was always proud of the childhood training he got from his mother. Mr. Solomon promised the mother that he will never depart from it as long as he lives.Sister Mary interrupted his husband by sayingit's on records that she had breastfed her husband more than her fifteen children combined, the past sixteen years.

Mr. Solomon suggested that since both of them were god-fearing, Sister Mary should also do for him what Sister Sarah Abraham did forBrother Abraham Terah by giving to him their maid to do what she could no longer do, just as Sarah gave Hagar to Abraham to do what Sarah couldn't do at the time.

Sister Mary resigned to her fate by conceding to continuing Mr. Solomon's daily breastfeeding program not minding the implications, in order to fulfil their marriage vows. The maid vanished from the house the following day — of course, you could tell what transpired after Mr. Solomon and Sister Mary's conversation. None of us realized that Santa heard and understood all these talks while they lasted, considering the fact that he was less than a day old— and was determined to put up a fight.

It was revealed on the eighth day that the child's name, as instructed by an angel, was Lucas (his real name), and Santa (his pen name).

However, Bro. Solo, together with Sis. Mary unanimously testified that an angel appeared to them in a concurrent and simultaneous vision of the night after I had prayed and Sis. Mary got pregnant, which was confirmed by their doctor that she was pregnant with a male child, just as the prophet had said. It was revealed through their testimony that the angel introduced himself as the "Morning Star" promised to all New World Citizens as recorded in the Holy Bible in the book of Revelations 2:28! According to them, he said that he was specially sent, because they, having overcome, were both expecting their first son. Both shared that the child's expected delivery time was revealed by the said angel which actually agreed with the doctor's prediction, which was 30th of November, but that he also had power to delay his delivery until 25th of December; only if they will give assent to his proposal. The condition was that their son should be called after him — Santa Claus, pointing to them how special their son will be, having been born on a Christmas day. He told them that he was the true Father Christmas, and that Christmas was his devoted day, since it was originated by him for his adherents through his vassals. That the child should always be called Santa, it being it's pet name. They continued by saying that the angel wanted their son to be called Lucas which is Latin for Luke, as the child will also grow to become a great writer and healer. Even you will believe such a revelation to have come from God having heard all that the angel said, considering the fact that they caught the vision simultaneously — at the same time of the night.

Chapter 2

Santa's Training.

And the child was named according to the angel's instruction having been born on the 25th of December just as he claimed he had power to do which was contrary to the medical prognosis, and the parents agreement on the day that it was born. Sister Mary kept all her promises to exclusivelybreastfeed Santa for four years. Thanks to grace, for God saw her plight.Breastfeeding Bro. Solo and Baby Santa concurrently is commendable, and award winning streak.

Santa had exclusive breastfeeding for four whole years. I can't decipher the source of the milk. Everything which involves Santa is just a miracle—if it was milk Santa was still getting from her mother's breast.Santa's mother began the second phase of her son's breastfeeding program which was inclusive, although it was short lived due to Bro. Solo's objection. Bro. Solo got the scheme terminated when Santa was six, implying that Santa had just two years of inclusive breastfeeding making a total of six years of persistent breastfeeding. Thanks to virtuous women like Sister Mary. It was because Santa had demanded absolute control of her mother's breast when he was six years old that gave rise to the internal crisis, and Bro. Solo's insistence that Santa was grown up, and that he should be confined to his own room which led to Santa's temporary defeat.

However, Sister Mary maintained that she must fulfill her promise to breastfeed Santa for eight years as a faithful Christian she was, citing Psalms 15:4;

"in whose eyes a vile man is despised, but who honors those who fear the LORD; he who keeps an oath even when it hurts, and doesn't change;"(Jewish Bible Complete).

She said her promise to breastfeed Bro. Solo was as well valid. It was bad news for Both Bro. Solo and Baby Santa as they had wanted to exercise absolute monopoly of Sister Mary's. Her priority was to train Santa in ways he should never depart from as he gets old just the same way Bro. Solo was trained by his own mother — a very good husband and devoted Christian. Sister Mary will always look forward to the day Baby Santa will grow up and also marry a good woman, suchlike her.

Mhhhhhhhhhhh!!!!!!!!!!!!

Santa Is Kidnapped.

It was because Santa won't succumb to his father's intimidations until he had completed his own training, thathis father was forced to arrange for the kidnap of his competitive son. It was such a woeful day for Sister Mary as Santa's kidnap took its toll on her health. Bro. Solo could not enjoy uninterrupted services that day as supposed due to Sister Mary's ailment because of Santa's kidnap. How frustrated Bro. Solo was at this stage of his life. Nothing he did that was contrary to Santa ever paid-off. And Santa always emerged the undisputed winner. May you be like Santa. The kidnappers were signaled early the following day by Bro. Solo to return their kidnappee, so as to avert the loss of Sister Mary. It was such a memorable day to the Solos as it was the first that Sister Mary was ever left to take care of herself by Bro. Solo. It was the first and only day that Sister Mary could not breastfeed Bro. Solo during their twenty two years of marriage. It was really her only conjugal leaf.

Santa, being older and wiser than his father knew via telegnosis that his father arranged for his kidnap, demanded that his mother buy him a toy gun that looked much like his father's revolver, which his mother did, and both agreed to keep it a secret though Sister Mary wasn't privy to Santa's plans.

Santa Waylays His Father.

One certain day, Bro. Solo upon returning home from business was met at the door by Santa with his toy gun his mother bought for him, while his wife was discharging some domestic chores at the kitchen.

"Your life, or your bedroom " was Santa's terms put forth to his father. Bro. Solo being one who wasn't just ready for any threatening drama, and thinking that Santa was using his revolver against him, since he had showed Santa where it was kept, and how to use it in the event that some hoodlums attacked their home; opted for his life at the expense of his marriage rights for the day, thus, was ushered into Santa's room, and shut in by his son. All this happened in the sitting room while Sis. Mary was busy with chores in the kitchen. Had she been at the door to welcome her husband, he won't have been so humiliated and imprisoned in his own house by his son. This left Santa with none to contend with for the day.

Moreover, Santa took possession of his father's phones, and briefcase and handed same to his mother, while also telling her that his father wants to have some quiet time, thus should be left alone until he's out by himself; that being the case was reason for the choice of his (Santa's) room. Furthermore, Santa remarked that his mother should encourage his father to make that a new habit as it was so surprising and worthy of commendations. Sister Mary was full of awe since it was the first time in the duration of their marriage that her husband was demanding to be left alone, hence, will do everything to encourage him. She quickly adjudged that her husband was now beginning to attain higher spirituality, thus was more mindful of spiritual exercises than sensual. So, Sister Mary never went anywhere near Santa's door all through the evening into the night until she had gone to bed. Santa's masterful scheme had paid off, while that of Bro. Solo failed. Santa had her mother all alone. It was the first time Sister Mary discharged her motherly duties to her six years old son without his father's interruption. It was such a development she considered good and groundbreaking, which will gladden anyone in her shoes! Maybe, she did testify in church the next worship service.

Bro. Solo, having been released the following day after his twelve hours house detention by his son could not let the cat out of the bag, even after he'd discovered that Santa's gun wasn't his short gun, but a toy gun his mother bought for him a few days ago. Too horrible! The same day, Bro. Solo sought for spiritual help from me because he'd just realized that he can't defeat Santa without divine intervention, and that I was a conduit to it, and could as well facilitate such intervention. It dawned on him that Santa was actually older than his birthday.

All he could tell me was that Santa had equalized. It was time for Santa's deliverance, he exclaimed. I retorted by saying that Santa doesn't need a second deliverance as he was already delivered six years ago when the angel visited them, and they acted in line with the angel's directives. I told him that Santa was acting under the influence of the purported morning star, the angelic being which appeared to them while Sister Mary was heavy with Santa. I had always known that Santa was negatively paranormal, but could not say so to avoid being seen as a sarcastic fellow, who is envious of people's progress especially, with regards to their angelic vision. I have long waited for this day. Thanks to all goodness it finally dawned.

Santa must reveal his true identity and source!

Santa Reveals His True Identity.

In order to not breed suspicion on Santa's mind, thereby, giving him a clue for what we're about to do, I had to go to their home for the deliverance exercise which was started casually, and without prior notice.

When I sang "wonder working power by the blood of the lamb"; and "anointing breaks the yoke", Santa warned me sternly that I had no legal right to do whatever I was poised to doing in his home. He claimed that Iwon't achieve any success by casting him out of his home because such actions outrightly negates God's laws and order! When I charged and proddedfurther to know the reasons for his claims, his response was so appalling, and worth more than a million dollar in cash. What follows is the case with most people who give room to Satan who assumes total control of their lives, and yet, expect to be free of him.

Santa's Exposé.

Santa revealed that after myprayer for the mother which led to her conceiving him, his parents were met by his agent who works at the hospital as an obstetrician/gynecologist where she registered for antenatal. After my agent doctor had predicted my birthday, I followed them to the house, after which I appeared to both of them simultaneously as an angel of light with the name as "Morning Star". It's actually my name which is translated as Lucifer. You can find me in Isaiah 14:12; Revelations 2:28; Job 38:7; 2Peter 1:19; etc.

Susceptibility And Gullibility Of Christians.

Santa continued by saying that he's the dawn of every civilization, citing "Job 38:7

"when the morning stars sang together, and all the sons of God shouted for joy?"

Jewish Bible Complete."

He said that most Christians can't discern his activities, operations, manifestations, revelations, or those that originate with him, because he's the "Morning Star"!

"I am the Morning Star because I'm the Light Bearer!

I am Lucifer!

I am Santa!

I amSatan!

Whenever I show up I do so as an angel of light, thereby, deceiving you gullible Christians, irrational andwonder lustcreatures who can't simplythink, nor use their priceless brains to reason with; but cheaply believe everything they see, or are told. You simpletons don't even consider the fact that I have been permitted by the Lord to perform certain wonders through my agents — the prophets. I have very many prophets among your clergy whose sole aim is to glorify me by promoting my propositions. The Lord said so in His discourses as recorded in the gospels and the apocalypse regarding the end times. "Matthew 24:11

"Many false prophets will arise, and will lead many astray."

Jewish Bible Complete."

"Matthew 24:24

"For there will arise false messiahs, and false prophets, and they will show great signs and wonders, so as to lead astray, if possible, even the chosen ones."

Jewish Bible Complete.""

Also citing Revelations chapters 13—17 as his strong reasons, etc.

Santa also said: "I don't just transform into an angel of light according to Paul's assertion in"2 Corinthians 11:14

"And no wonder, for even Satan masquerades as an angel of light."

Jewish Bible Complete",

because I was created a light bearer from the beginning of my being, until I perverted Divine Truths that made me bright.

"Ezekiel 28:13

"You were in Eden, the garden of God. Every precious stone adorned you"

Ezekiel 28:14

"You were the anointed cherub who covers. Then I set you up on the holy mountain of God. You have walked up and down in the middle of the stones of fire."

Ezekiel 28:15

"You were perfect in your ways from the day that you were created, until unrighteousness was found in you."

Ezekiel 28:16

"By the abundance of your commerce, your insides were filled with violence, and you have sinned. Therefore I have cast you as profane out of God's mountain. I have destroyed you, covering cherub, from the middle of the stones of fire."

Ezekiel 28:17

"Your heart was lifted up because of your beauty. You have corrupted your wisdom by reason of your splendor. I have cast you to the ground. I have laid you before kings, that they may see you."

Jewish Bible Complete".

I still have the truth, but it's perverted and can be found among most of you Christians.That's why I deceive most of you without hassle. It's my kind of truth that the Lord calls Lie in John 8:44.

I pervert every good thing which comes from above, including many false teachings all through the ages!

Only the Greater Light can overshadow and overpower me, but, not in this case because these people accepted me wholeheartedly: and Godwon't violate their rights, nor overrule and overturn their choices and decisions which are a sacred trust bestowed on them by their maker, as long as it doesn't hurt others without their consent"".

The Price Of Dereliction.

"You all are derelicts!

Mental derelicts!

Civil derelicts

Spiritual derelicts!

Psychological derelicts!

Intellectual derelicts!

Political derelicts!

Economic derelicts!

Irredeemable poor derelicts!

That is why most of you are poorer than the poor among my people! You sell out cheaply, only to come back for a fight when I'm already established, and it's too late for you to succeeded because you can't live long enough to fight me through to success."

Then I charged in the name of Jesus Christ to know what actually transpired because I strongly believed that God gave the child after I'd prayed for the Solo's. Santa's response was so appalling that I could not grasp it at the time.

Santa confessed : "It all happened when they believed I was the messenger of God and adopted my suggested names, and date of birth to coincide with Christmas day.

"So, what is in the name; Santa and Lucas?" I asked. Isn't Santa meant to be short form for Santa Claus — also known as Father Christmas? """

Santa laughed at me scornfully. "Ignorant Christians! " Santa exclaimed. "You senseless folks sheepishly adopt names, practices, dates and days, and teachings in utter ignorance of their origin, and meanings, and whom they're traceable to. Once adopted, such glue easily to you and become your most cherished and propagated doctrines which promote my kingdom, while also being admired as your own religion. Clueless fools — I wish the Lord will leave me alone to have you all in my kingdom stealthily through my agents, teachings, and practices, in my ancient wisdom. No wonder that the Lord said that my children are wiser than you Christians; citing: Luke 16:8

""His lord commended the dishonest manager because he had done wisely, for the children of this world are, in their own generation, wiser than the children of the light."

Jewish Bible Complete".

Santa Is an Anagram Of Satan.

"Let me tell you, you ignoramus "; Santa continued:

"SANTA is an anagram of SATAN.

LUCAS is an anagram of CLAUS.

You fools should also know that CLAUS is an acrostic for:

C — Christmas

L — Lovers

A — Are

U — Under

S — Satan.

"Christmas Lovers Are Under Satan"."""

Incredible indeed.

The Origin Of Christmas.

Santa Claus claimed and proved to me that he was truly "Father Christmas ", or the originator of it. He said that father means the source, generator, author, beginner, pioneer, or originator of a thing, or place. That all who cherished and celebrated Santa Claus and his day, did so to him.

Santa's Vassal.

Santa revealed that he accomplished the Christmas day celebration feat through his vassal on the earth whom he planted in the church through feigned conversion when he realized that Christianity was invincibly and rapidly becoming a global movement. The only way for him to remain relevant was to join the holy ones and infiltrate them by introducing his own teachings, practices, holy days, etc. That was a monumental success that will last for as long as time. He said that he foresaw a time in the future when all his adherents may forsake him for the worship of the true Lord, as was already being done every Passover, now called Easter. He entered into the church through her leaders whom the congregants upheld as holy, sacred, infallible, and choice divine vessels with unquestionable authority; and that he took advantage of a prophecy, citing "Isaiah 3:12

"As for my people, children are their oppressors, and women rule over them. My people, those who lead you cause you to err, and destroy the way of your paths."

Jewish Bible Complete".

So, Santa introduced his own day to be celebrated amongst Christians just as they celebrated Christ during Easter. He vehemently affirmed that Christmas was both technically and legally his day, and everyone who celebrates the day does so in worship of him. He concluded by bidding me with firm conviction to verify from Emperor Constantine, his vassal at the time.

Christmas Is Santa's Holy Day.

Santa went on charging me to prove from the Holy Bible where it says that the Jesus Christ who we supposedly celebrate on Christmas day was born that day. But, he could prove to me that history was on his side — Christmas day actually being an ancient pagan ceremonial day introduced to Christianity through Satan's wisdom so as to have all Christians worshipping him universally in ignorance of the days actual history, as though they worshipped the Lord Jesus Christ.

Santa's audacious claims surpassed my faith when he sternly warned that I desist from meddling with his family's affairs, and his businesses wherever he was gladly received, appreciated, and hosted. Santa asserted that this family loved him so much, though in ignorance of his true identity, by adopting his dates and names — that also being Adam and Eve's cause of failure. He disclosed that this family rejected God given child in exchange for him once they acted in line with his guidance. Accepting his suggestions implied replacing him instead of the child God gave to them when I prayed.

I declared to him that he was a blatant liar, as he could not be real except that he possessed the boy's body. With this I have found new grounds to anchor my faith and subsequently dislodge him.

What follows is really interesting.

Chapter 3

The Power Of Habits

Habits can be a man's prison, just as can bring him freedom.

Habits are the creators of our success, or failures ecosystem.

Our habits define our habitat.

In suit, habits are our prisons. They soon conquer us once they are formed by us. Habits are our creations which tend to destroy us than any other of our inventions.

Our habits are deistic. They aren't evil in themselves, but are a reflection of our past lives.

Neither God, nor Satan, influences our habits, but either waxes, or wanes in us by our habits.

Habits are the building blocks of our destinies. Our habits are the feeders of good, or evil. They are the soil upon which trees of acts grow to yield commensurate fruits which we must undoubtedly reap some day.

Before you accuse another of being responsible for your ordeals in life, check your habits. What do they inhibit, or enhance? If your habits are such that inhibit success, not even God who can do all things will make you succeed in life except you change your failure enhancing habits.

Our habits are either conductors, or insulators, depending on the materials they are made up of. They can conduct either life or death, success or failure, etc.

Habitat simply means living at your habit — habit—at. So, your placement in life is a function of your daily habits. You can't grow beyond your habitual thinking patterns. You can't be richer than your earning and spending habits. You can't be healthier than your health habits.

You are as good, or as bad as your habits.

You're as rich, or as poor as your habits.

You're as strong and healthy, or as weak and sickly as your habits.

Your habits are either the builders, or destroyers of your life, not witchcraft. As a matter of fact, your habits are the conduit through which they affect your life. No devil can stand a chance against good and life enriching habits.

A good life is a function of good daily habits. Same applies to a poor life.

Habits are so faithful that they are inclined to only attract their kinds.

Your life is a just reward for your past habits.

One may ask, but what of the devil and his evil work?Doesn't he afflict people?

The devil is in your habits. He destroys through habits. He afflicts through habits.

God is also in habits. He builds, or comforts through habits.

Good habits are godly, while evil habits are devilish.

Our habits resonate more than our prayers, even when praying seems to be our habits.

The crux of the revelation was after Santa had revealed that his mother has been training him to become a habitual sucker who will even do betterthan his father is, because he must fulfil Proverbs 22:6 which says:

""Train up a child in the way he should go, and when he is old he will not depart from it."

Jewish Bible Complete", also citing John 10:35; and Mark 13:31

Yochanan 10:35

"If he called them gods, to whom the word of God came (and the Scripture can't be broken),"

Jewish Bible Complete

Mark 13:31

"Heaven and earth will pass away, but my words will not pass away."

Jewish Bible Complete"""".

He stood his ground, yelling that he must fulfil scriptures this time, at least for once in his lifetime. I took the exit door, having been clearly whipped by seemingly little Santa, as he had been given so much rights in this family. I turned around and began to retrace my steps back to my house.

Now that Bro. Solo and Sis. Mary have known the true identity of Santa, that will make them willingly accept my next courses ofstrategicactions, at least with regards to Santa as he has been untouchable since his birth. Not even God would have been allowed to touch Santa prior to this day by the Solos.

The Futility Of Human Folly.

I suggested to Bro. Solo that since he's the owner of his wife's body according to

Scriptures, he should compound a mixture of marched vinegar, together with every extremely bitter, but nonlethal herbs which he knows, and anoint her wife's mammary with it; thinking that will repel Santa, thereby terminating Santa's presence in his bedroom when he taste it, citing 1 Corinthians 7:1—5. That turned out to give Santa an unfair advantage over his father that day. We discovered through that that Santa's taste buds were as paranormal as his character. We failed woefully because Santa had his best day ever, as his father could not stand the bitter taste of Sister Mary's breast. Bro. Solo have just become Santa's fan in his own his, and over his own legally married wife.

Be Wise As Serpents.

Having been whipped again together with Bro. Solo by Santa, I resorted to consult the Lord on the issue while also retracting my previous counsel which gave Santa an indisputable lead over his father. The Lord chided me for ever thinking that I could meet the devil and whip him at the level of human wisdom. He revealed that humanistic thinkingcan't be a match to thedevil's thinking, as the devil can as well be found in humanistic thinking.He's been in the game long before man was. The Lord told me that I could only stand on the same plane with Satan when I become wise as serpent, and will defeat him when I operate at the frequency of divine wisdom.

"Matthew 10:16

""Behold, I send you out as sheep among wolves. Therefore be wise as serpents, and harmless as doves."

Jewish Bible Complete

Luke 21:15

"for I will give you a mouth and wisdom which all your adversaries will not be able to withstand or to contradict."

Jewish Bible Complete"".

The Lord was so merciful thatbestowed wisdom to emerge victorious in this battle to me, and it paid-off, at last.

Wisdom To Rout And Roust Evil.

The Lord revealed that the evil one took charge of Santa's lifethrough the adoption of his suggested names, and that deliberately changing the name will change the effect and influence of Satan on his life. He said that everyone answers to their names, and that names determine who, or, what controls a person, place, or thing.

Immediately, I went to Bro. Solo's home and declared God's counsel for them concerning Santa's liberation from Satan's possession, which was gladly received by all, but Santa. I would condone his excesses owing to the fact that he was under the influence of Satan. That's why he's Santa. However, Santa was of the opinion that his mother persistently rob the compound prepared by his father on her breasts, but should never accept the change of his name I imposed on them, citing

Ecclesiastes 3:14

"I know that whatever God does, it shall be forever. Nothing can be added to it, nor anything taken from it; and God has done it, that men should fear before him."

Jewish Bible Complete.

Then I cited Genesis 35:18:

"As her soul was departing (for she died), she named him Benoni, but his father named him Benjamin."

Jewish Bible Complete.

Also, Genesis 2:19

"Out of the ground the LORD God formed every animal of the field, and every bird of the sky, and brought them to the man to see what he would call them. Whatever the man called every living creature became its name."

Jewish Bible Complete.

Santa mocked, and scuffed, saying: " should you successfully free him from being possessed by me through changing his names, will you also change their habits which are as old as they are? You can't change their lives except you change their habits which were formed through childhood parental training.I'll continue to live in their habits because they are such that empowers me. But you know that they are habituated to daily suckling program, and I am in that. Will you also exorcise the habit in them considering the fact that the were accumulated and formed rigorously through many years of training? I found this window of opportunity and seized it, then it became my habitat. Until the habit goes, he remains my habitation, since I live and habits, and habits are in people. Habits are my habitats! He yelled.

There shall nothing be impossible with God, and to the believer, I retorted. So, I changed Santa's name to Solomon (Jnr.), since he's more like his father habitually.

Both God And Satan Feed Through Our Habits.

One of Santa's amazing revelation was that many who claim to be Christians were not, because he lives and feeds through them by their evil habits. Any habit one has built over time has either him, or the Lord living and feeding in, and through it. So, you must be careful of your personal training scheme — which is habit building.

How People Become Gays, Lesbians, Bisexuals, And Heterosexuals.

Furthermore, Santa revealed that when female babies are given exclusive breastfeeding, and are accustomed to being nursed andpampered by their mothers, or other female folks, they'll grow up to be habitual seekers of female pampering, and the result will be lesbianism.

If she was raised, orpampered by both sexes, she'll be inclined to heterosexualism.

If a male child was raised, or pampered by fellow males, the result will be gayism. Now you know how people become gay in life and the origin of homosexuality.

If the father alone raises, or pampers his daughters with the mother inclusively breastfeeding them, the girls will grow up to be decent women who will stick to only their husbands all their lives, since that 's how they were trained. If the mother alone trains a male child with inclusive breastfeeding, the boy will grow up to be a decent man who will glue to his wife aloneall his life modestly.

Satan's Contemporary Vassals.

Santa disclosed that he used his contemporary vassals in the field of medicine to promote exclusive breastfeeding so as to raise vampire breast suckers, and child rights laws to train many homosexuals in their own homes by their parents/guardians.

Finally, Santa opted to join his siblings abroad after over three years of resistance when his father suggested that he joined them then, having been completely whipped by me this time round. Before leaving, Santa asked to know if his future wife will be as magnanimous as his mother has been... From that you can easily decipher what Santa was already contemplating. So, Santa was finally free to live his life modestly, and without any external influence.

The next line of action will be how to rid Santa of his six years old habit of daily breast sucking. It's a task that must be accomplished before he's of a marriageable age, else, we have another sucking demon to contend with — who knows if it will be you, or your daughter, or your sister, niece, or your cousin? It may as well be that your enemy, or one of their daughters that will be getting married to Santa. Just think about that and start praying passionately that God will deliver your daughters from Santa's bondage, because it promises to be greater than that of Bro. Solo having exceeded him by two more years of uninterrupted training.

Bro. Solo is already enjoying my teachings on soberness, self-control, fasting and prayer, etc.; although I can't measure the degree of corresponding effect on his life yet, since Sister Mary may never mention that any significant change has occurred as she was already feeling relieved with Santa's absence, for she was used to serving two masters simultaneously without feeling any weight. That was what defined her feminity. At least her burdens now seems to be relieved.

Parents! What are you training your children to become in life, knowing that they won't depart from it, since even Satan knows that the scriptures can't be broken?

Satan, through Santa mentioned that he was in so many homes training his army of soldiers through their parents, just as he's in so many churches training his eternal tenants through the clergy by his doctrines and practices, or lack of it.

Mark 13:37

"What I tell you, I tell all"

Jewish Bible Complete".

The King James Version adds "watch"!

1 Peter 5:8

"Be sober and self-controlled. Be watchful. Your adversary, the devil, walks around like a roaring lion, seeking whom he may devour."

Jewish Bible Complete.

Habits: Habitats For Good, Or Evil.

Just as I said earlier based on Santa's revelations, I decided to take my leave when I got a stunning response from Santa who introduced himself as habit, yelling that he can't leave Solomon (Jnr.) as long as he was scripturally trained by his mother to be a suckling demon — that leaving will negate the authority of the scriptures. Having commanded habit to leave in the name of Jesus Christ — habit insisted that he must stay as long as Solomon (Jnr.) needs him, and that God has magnified His word above all His names, citingPsalms 138:2. He claimed that as long as Proverbs 22:6 was a divine law, and he was acting in accordance with

God's law, all my efforts will be futile irrespective of whatever name I invoked to cast him out pointing to Jesus Christ as being God's Word in John Gospel 1:1—3; and Revelations 19:13; 1 John 5:7.

I cited Matthew 16:19; 18:18—19; hence, I agreed with Bro. Solo and Sister Mary in prayer that habit must go. Finally, habit was also dislodge having been humiliated, but vowed to return for reprisals so as to reclaim his old habitat when Santa is of marriageable age since he's been training for that age through the memories of his childhood.

Yochanan 5:14

"Afterward Yeshua found him in the temple, and said to him, "Behold, you are made well. Sin no more, so that nothing worse happens to you.""

Jewish Bible Complete.

Right now, Santa (Solomon {Jr.}) is undergoing reformational training to renew his mind, in order to transform into a new man. We're also contemplating preparing him for priesthood where here can ultimately avoid marriage and go the way of celibates — which, of course may not be God's purpose for his life, just to keep women from imminent danger.

What do you think should be done to Santa, in order to save his future knowing he's a potential terrorist raised by his over caringmother who was lured into agreement by his father?

Chapter 4.

Santa's   Eschatological Enquiries.

Sister Mary was so excited when Santa told her that he will love to preach the

Gospel of Jesus Christ. She got even more elated when Santa said that the subject of eternity was his most preferred in the entire Holy Scriptures, and that he would like to live eternally with the Lord Jesus Christ in heaven, but, for a few issues which are unacceptable to him. Sister Mary's response was affirmative when Santa mentioned that he understood that eternity was forever.

More so, Santa revealed that he found the all important scriptural subject of "The Lord's Marriage Supper absolutely repugnant.

The conversation went this way:

Santa: will father also be married to Jesus Christ in the marriage supper?

Sister Mary: Yes!

Santa: will Jesus Christ marry me also?

Sister Mary: Yes!

Santa: Will Jesus Christ marry you too?

Sister Mary: Yes!

Will Jesus Christ marry all my sisters?

Sister Mary: Yes!

Santa: Will Jesus Christ marry everyone in the Church?

Sister Mary: Yes!

Santa: How could Jesus Christ do such a thing? You mean he'll be the only husband in heaven?

You mean that only Jesus Christ will marry all the men, women, children in the church? Why will he do such a thing. Is He the only one that wants to marry?

Don't He pity and love us anymore?

Is that why He wants all of us to go to heaven so he can exercise marriage monopoly?

Sister Mary: Because Jesus Christ is the Lord of all and the Head of the Church which is His body.

Santa: When I get to the States, I'll askPresident Donald Trump to leave LGBTs alone, since there will be gay marriage in heaven, and Jesus Christ is gay because He'll marry all the men in heaven including me. I'll show him where that is written in the Holy Bible since he now claims that he's also a Christian. I'll let President Trump to know that he too will be married to Jesus Christ if he gets to heaven, and both he and Jesus Christ are men — which is gay marriage.

Santa continued: I'll also ask father to marry more wives since Jesus Christ will marry many wives in heaven, and the Solomon he was named after married very many wives according to the Bible. Mother, what do you think about father marrying many more women?"

Sister Mary was bereft of words.

Santa: I'll tell the Pastor to start preaching support for, and wed LGBTs, Polygamy, Pedophilia, etc.

Sister Mary: Why will you say such a thing? That is blasphemous, and is punishable under the law of God, by eternal damnation in hell fire with the devils.

Santa: That is because you don't understand Scriptures the way I do. For instance, what is polygamy? It is marrying more than one wife. And Jesus will marry everyone in heaven which is uncountable wives — that is polygamy.

Jesus Christ will marry all the men in heaven — that is polygamous gay marriage.

Jesus Christ will marry all the women in heaven — that is polygamous solomony.

Jesus Christ will marry all the children in heaven — that is polygamous Pedophilia.

Jesus Christ will transform all the men and boys in heaven into women so he can marry them as a man — that is polygamous transsexuality.

Jesus Christ will marry all the men and boys and women alike in heaven — that is polygamous bisexuality.

Is Jesus Christ hermaphrodite to have possessed both male and female genital organs at the same time?

That will be too much for Him alone. Solomon could not manage his one thousand well that he backslider, won't Jesus Christ also backslide in heaven thereby offending God just like Solomon?I'll tell Jesus Christ to allow me help him with some after all we're friends, and what are friends for?

Santa May Have Relapsed...

"Why would Jesus Christ be the only husband in heaven?

Why should he marry all the women alone?

Why shouldn't He allow father and I to also marry in heaven women in heaven, or, is He the only one who likes and deserves good things?

Didn't He teach that we should love and be our brothers keeper by sharing our possessions with them?Didn't Jesus Christ teach in the Holy Bible that we should love our neighbors, including our enemies just as we love ourselves?

But mother, isn't Jesus Christ being selfish by claiming all the good things of life to himself alone?

Sister Mary: What are these good things of life?

Santa: All the beautiful and caring women like you.

Maybe, it's because it is His heaven. And I'd rather not go there, except you and father will marry my own wife for me now so that before I get to Jesus' heaven I must have benefitted a lot. Maybe, I shouldn't even go to Jesus' heaven so he won't seize my beautiful and caring wife for me, else, I'll fighthim.

Upon Bro. Solo's return, Santa welcomed him with the following questions:

Santa: father, is it true that you and mother won't be marrying in heaven?

Bro. Solo: Yes, my son.

Santa: Is it true that you and mother will marry Jesus Christ instead in heaven?

BRl. Solo: Yes.

Santa: How will you cope in heaven without having mother as your wife in heaven?

You'd betterstart training yourself for that here, so, you'll be used to it before you get to heaven, in order to not fight Jesus the way you used to fight with me.I'll congratulate Jesus Christ, as I also direct mother to commence your training for heaven tonight. If you don't commence your training tonight you'll go to hell fire, because Jesus Christ doesn't condone rivalry with anyone in his heaven. See how He dealt with the devils.

Bro. Solo: Why would you say a thing like that?

Santa: Because you and Pastor connived to make mother stop breastfeeding me. Now you have it all to yourself alone. Enjoy, knowing that your time and that of the devils is very short. Keep colonizing mother now. Jesus will also colonize her in heaven and you'll just be watching. Very soon your monopoly, and lease will expire, and both of us will be at the same level again. Father, go to your own mother and leave my mother for me alone. I have never contended for your mother with you. Leave my mother alone, as he continued his rants in protest.

Was Santa ever delivered, or, maybe he just relapsed?

Chapter 5

Santa's Theosophy.

One certain day, Santa was so elated to share with us a revelation he claimed to have received from an angel who introduced himself to him as he that "LIVED".

However, I'm repugnant to his claims because I know that "LIVED" may as well be an anagram for "DEVIL" just as "SANTA" is for "SATAN"; even though Santa believes that the being must be the Lord Jesus Christ because he had stigmata on his body.

It had been said of old that experience is the best teacher, but, I say to you that instruction is the best teacher, because one might not live long enough to recover from certain experiences in this life — get instructions from the Bible.

The End Of Eden, And The Rise Of Babylon.

According to Santa's revelation, all animals, fishes, and birds that have tails, have it behind, or attached to their backside — while only men who are higher mammals have theirs attached to their front side. Do you want to know why?

You better follow up with Santa'smind-blowing and eye opening revelation.

Why Men Have Their Tails In Front.

Santa claims that it's sin that's responsible for man wearing his tail in front, unlike other animals.

The tail of every man is a reminder of the consequence of Adam's sin— hence, men must desist from further sinning.

God made man in His own image, and put him in the garden of Eden as its manager. He was commanded to not eat of the fruit of a certain tree — you know the remaining part of the story.

In those days, serpents were the wisest, and most beautiful of all god—created animals. They looked like the hinds (female Red Deer). Genesis 3:1

"Now the serpent was more subtle than any animal of the field which the LORD God had made. He said to the woman, "Has God really said, 'You shall not eat of any tree of the garden'?""

Jewish Bible Complete.

Genesis 3:14

"The LORD God said to the serpent, "Because you have done this, you are cursed above all livestock, and above every animal of the field. You shall go on your belly and you shall eat dust all the days of your life."

Jewish Bible Complete.

Serpents had horns and hooves.

Men didn't have front tails, nor women have twin fruits on their chest. A day came when the human physiology will change for ever.

A day came when the serpent being the most beautiful and wisest of all the animals, was able to convince the woman and her man to eat of the other fruit — from the forbidden tree — even the tree of death. So, God was angry with them, and decided to punish all of them for flouting His eternal law.

In order to punish the serpent in a measure that corresponds to the degree of its sin, God detached its limbs which had hooves, and its tail from its physical body, leaving only the twin horns on its head which were transformed into spiritual and invisible to the naked eyes. That is why serpents no longer have limbs, tails, and physical horns like every other cattle. So, the once most beautiful animal became a creeper which now drags itself on the dust of the earth.

For the man, God said that his sins must go before him. And in punishing the man for his sins, God attached the hindlike tail of the serpent which He had detached from it to the man. That 'show men began to wear frontal tails. It isn't a free gift of God, but, the wages of his sins. To prove the severity of the punishment due to the gravity of his offence, God didn't fix the tail where other mammals wear theirs, but in front, so that man will always see it and remember to always flee from evil and all its semblances. So, all men's sins are designed by God to go before them — I mean the frontal tail — I don't know what you call it.

1 Timothy 5:24

"Some men's sins are evident, preceding them to judgment, and some also follow later."

Jewish Bible Complete.

1 Timothy 5:25

"In the same way also there are good works that are obvious, and those that are otherwise can't be hidden."

Jewish Bible Complete.

As for the hindlike feet of the serpent which God detached from its body, He projected them into the spiritual body of man, so that man will use them to bruise the head of the serpent, while the serpent will bruise his heel — this actually happens spiritually.

Genesis 3:15

"I will put hostility between you and the woman, and between your offspring and her offspring. He will bruise your head, and you will bruise his heel.""

(Jewish Bible Complete).

It's because of the foregoing, that the man said in Psalms 18:33:

"He makes my feet like deer's feet, and sets me on my high places."

(Jewish Bible Complete), to enable the man to trample upon serpents as a reprisal for making him to be published with its tail. This is one of the many reasons why man's frontal tail is a pleasurelust machine. God said that he won't take away the serpent's horns so they will be thorns in man's flesh whenever it bruises man's heel.

Numbers 33:55

""But if you do not drive out the inhabitants of the land from before you, then those you let remain of them will be like pricks in your eyes and thorns in your sides. They will harass you in the land in which you dwell."

(Jewish Bible Complete).

Classes Of Men.

According to the Holy Scriptures, the most sinful men are called Egyptians. They have maximum sizes of tails.

Average sinful men are called Assyrians — they possess medium sizes of tails.

The least sinful men are called the Chaldeans, or the Babylonians. They wear the least or minimum sizes of tails. And you don't have to blame them if you're their wife. It's not a crime to be less sinful than others yet. Or, do you wish that God rewards them more than their sins weigh? God forbid.

Ezekiel 16:26

"You have also committed sexual immorality with the Egyptians, your neighbors, great of flesh; and have multiplied your prostitution, to provoke me to anger."

Ezekiel 16:27

"See therefore, I have stretched out my hand over you, and have diminished your portion, and delivered you to the will of those who hate you, the daughters of the Philistines, who are ashamed of your lewd way."

Ezekiel 16:28

"You have played the prostitute also with the Assyrians, because you were insatiable; yes, you have played the prostitute with them, and yet you weren't satisfied."

Ezekiel 16:29

"You have moreover multiplied your prostitution to the land of merchants, to

Kasdimah {Chaldea}; and yet you weren't satisfied with this."

(Jewish Bible Complete).

The truth is that the bigger a man's sin, the bigger the tail, for it is the wages of his sins. So, you know men by their tails.

Women And Their Twin Fruits.

And, for the woman who was the first to collaborate with the serpent, God doubled her punishment and made them more severe. But for love, God would have put them on her head. He put her own punishment on her bosom (chest), since the evil act came from that region — her heart.

Mark 7:21

"For from within, out of the hearts of men, proceed evil thoughts, adulteries, sexual sins, murders, thefts,"

(Jewish Bible Complete).

Concerning the woman, the Lord said: Psalms 128:3

"Your wife will be as a fruitful vine in the innermost parts of your house, your children like olive plants around your table."

(Jewish Bible Complete).

Also, Song Of Solomon 6:6

"Your teeth are like a flock of ewes, which have come up from the washing, of which every one has twins; not one is bereaved among them."

(Jewish Bible Complete).

This is the origin of 666 which is said to be the mark of the beast. The beast punishment is triple, hence, triple six (666)

The woman is next to Satan on the scale of sinfulness, hence hers is double six (66); even so the Scriptures which clearly captured God's pronouncement of the wages of her sins was SOS 6:6. They're dangerous. They're only second to the devil, and none else.

Now, in order to know what these teeth, which are twins mean, the Lord went further to say:

Song Of Solomon 4:5

"Your two breasts are like two fawns that are twins of a roe, which feed among the lilies."

(Jewish Bible Complete).

You Shall Know Them By Their Fruits.

The woman is as a fruitful vine, and that is why she was made to bear twin fruits on her bosom — they originally were of the devil. God detached them from the serpent and attached them to the woman. I mean the twin fruits — and none is barren — everyone bears twins — the dividends of sin. It is paid in doubles.

Just as is with the man, so it is with the woman.The size of their fruits is determined by the size of their sins — "for by their fruits you shall know them".

Matthew 7:16

"By their fruits you will know them. Do you gather grapes from thorns, or figs from thistles?"

(Jewish Bible Complete).

As their sins so is the sizes, says Santa.

Yochanan 10:35

"..., to whom the word of God came (and the Scripture can't be broken),"

Jewish Bible Complete).

So, according to Santa's revelation, you can now easily know the most sinful and less sinful among men an women by their fruits. You don't need any special gift or ability to do that.

Do you see what sin caused? Twin fruits for the woman, and frontal tail for the man, and yet, men and women won't stop sinning. They even sin more nowadays through the use of these their wages of sin.

So, I told Santa that the wages of sin is death, and that he'll die soon for enjoying her mothers fruit for so long. Santa quickly pointed to the father that he'll be the first to die since he'd been eating of those fruits since his childhood.

Bro. Solo won't say a word because he was culpable.

Why The Breast Is Called "MAMMARY".

Santa claimed that these two, the frontal tail in men and twins fruits in women have been responsible for more sins among men than any other part of their bodies, reason being that, these two originally belonged to the serpent.

Stop using them if you want to live long, is my candid advice to you all.

I have been told, that the woman is the highest mammal, that's why her fruits are near the head, and are called the "MAMMARY".

There's Liberty In Marriage.

Santa concluded his purported revelation by saying that he had been permitted to enjoy the MAMMARY and yet live. His only exemption route is marriage. That it's permitted for use only in marriage. That, when married, the woman is the mother of all the living just as Eve. But, when unmarried, she's the"MURDER" of all the living — that's when you enjoy her fruit outside marriage, you'll die like Adam.

Proverbs 6:26

"For a prostitute reduces you to a piece of bread. The adulteress hunts for your precious life."

Proverbs 6:32

"He who commits adultery with a woman is void of understanding. He who does it destroys his own soul."

(Jewish Bible Complete).

Now both the tail in man and the twin fruits in woman, when in marriage become instruments of life generation and preservation, and most importantly, health, and pleasures for evermore.

Your Opinion?

What do you think about Santa, and where to find him now in the States?

Kindly review and share your opinion with us.

Thank You so much for meeting here with us.

WATCH OUT FOR BOOK TWO IN THIS SERIES.

EBARIM, FORTUNE GODSEND.

About The Author:

Ebarim, Fortune Godsend is the pioneer Prime Minister of Edenlife Church Without Walls (A. K. A. New World Citizens) Judges 18:10; and the Founding President of Ebarim Fortune Godsend Global Ministries.He's also the Senior Pastor of Better life Worship Center — a nondenominational Christian gathering at Calabar, Cross River State, Nigeria.

His works speak for him, which are as follows: Don't Die Poor — Biblical Strategies For Success; The Little Foxes That Spoil The Vine; The Workshop Experience; The Believer's Divine Rights; Who Is In Your Boat?; Avoiding The Bitter Errors Of Righteous Job; Singled Out; Demystifying The Betrayal Of Christ; and lots more, many of which are in their audio and video formats not yet on the Amazon Platform.

He was born on the 27th of December, 1981, into the family of Mr. Bernard and Mrs. Justina Akparika Ndifon, both of Osomba Village in Akamkpa Local Government Area of Cross River State, Nigeria.

He's Still single.

Through several visions of the Lord Jesus Christ, his mandate in life, as said by the mouth of the Lord Jesus Christ himself, among others, is to: "Build The Ark, Raise New Kingdom MoneybagsWho WillBearThe Contents Of TheBag With AKingdomBuilding Consciousness, Empower and Transform Lives" by: "Persistently Teaching The Word OfLife, And Consistently Living And Manifesting The Supernatural Through The Holy Ghost And Faith Connection; A Threefold Cord Which Cannot Be Easily Broken..."

About The Book:

Brother Fortune seeks to express some of his heartfelt yearnings through this medium. Some are true revelations which were revealed to him by the Lord Jesus Christ himself. The characters here may be represented, and some fun introduced into the stories to shed light on the level of ignorance prevalent in the church which was ordained to be a light of the world.

This book reveals some practices in the church which have been made to be superior to the laws of the Lord himself.

Some doctrinal differences that exist today are still amendable only if we're willing.

Babylon is Santa's Empire, and Santa is the king of Babylon. He thrives by his means, the most useful of which is deception.

Watch! That's all I can say.

Bro. Fortune says :"Habits, once formed, either become our "god", or our devils. You might say that demons are responsible for your ordeals in life, but, it is truer that they only took advantage of, and thrived on your habits"".

Customs are habits. God is in them when they're good, and Satan is also in them when they're evil.

Meditate on that.

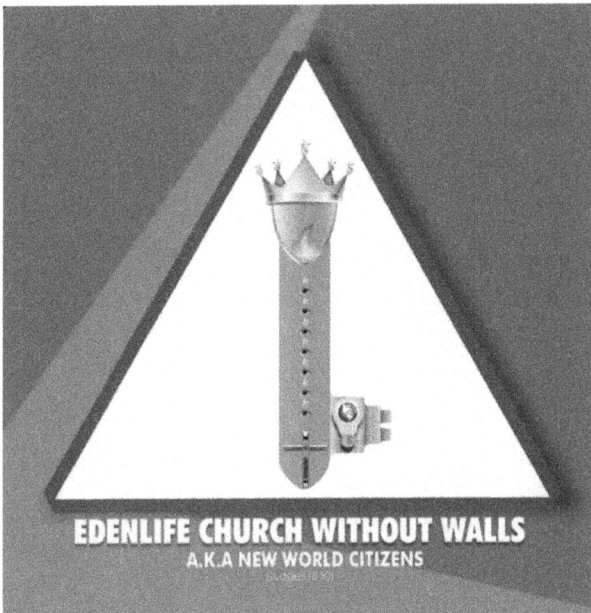

EDENLIFE CHURCH WITHOUT WALLS
A.K.A NEW WORLD CITIZENS